QUOKKAS

by Jaclyn Jaycox

PEBBLE

a capstone imprint

Pebble Explore is published by Pebble, an imprint of Capstone.
1710 Roe Crest Drive
North Mankato, Minnesota 56003
www.capstonepub.com

Library of Congress Cataloging-in-Publication Data
Names: Jaycox, Jaclyn, 1983- author.
Title: Quokkas / by Jaclyn Jaycox.
Description: North Mankato, Minnesota : Pebble, [2021] | Series: Animals |
  Includes bibliographical references and index. | Audience: Ages 5-8 |
  Audience: Grades 2-3 | Summary: "Quokkas might be the cutest animals
  you've never heard of. These furry little creatures look like a cross
  between a kangaroo and a squirrel. Get fun details about this adorable
  Australian animal"— Provided by publisher.
Identifiers: LCCN 2021002429 (print) | LCCN 2021002430 (ebook) | ISBN
  9781977132000 (hardcover) | ISBN 9781977133021 (paperback) | ISBN
  9781977154774 (pdf) | ISBN 9781977156433 (kindle edition)
Subjects: LCSH: Quokka—Juvenile literature.
Classification: LCC QL737.M35 J39 2021 (print) | LCC QL737.M35 (ebook) |
  DDC 599.2/2—dc23
LC record available at https://lccn.loc.gov/2021002429
LC ebook record available at https://lccn.loc.gov/2021002430

Image Credits
Alamy: Keith J Smith, 21; Capstone Press, 6; Newscom: jspix imageBROKER, 12, Kevin Schafer/ Minden Pictures, 11, 13; Shutterstock: Ashley Whitworth, 18, Benny Marty, 7, BigBoom, 5, ByWagner, 15, Damian Lugowski, 1, 10, 17, EA Given, 22, Grakhantsev Nikolai, Cover, John Crux, 27, Kompasskind.de, 28, LIMDQ, 8, Marie Henson, 25, Phoebe Burke, 14

Editorial Credits
Editor: Hank Musolf; Designer: Dina Her; Media Researcher: Morgan Walters; Production Specialist: Tori Abraham

All internet sites appearing in back matter were available and accurate when this book was sent to press.

Printed and bound in China.   4205

Table of Contents

Words in **bold** are in the glossary.

Amazing Quokkas

Say cheese! Quokkas are always smiling. Sometimes it's a small smirk. Other times it's a big, toothy grin! Because of this, they are called "the happiest animals on Earth."

These animals are a type of **mammal**. They have fur. They give birth to live young. They are in the **marsupial** family. They have pouches. Kangaroos and koalas are also in this family.

Where in the World

   Quokkas live in Australia. The largest group is on Rottnest Island. There are about 10,000 to 12,000 there. Smaller groups live on Bald Island and in western Australia.

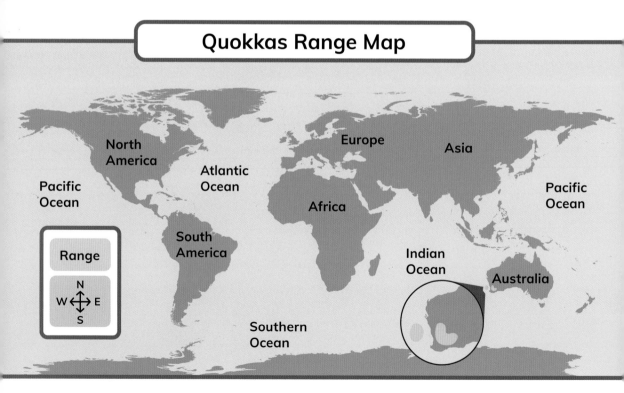

Quokkas Range Map

North America

Europe

Asia

Atlantic Ocean

Pacific Ocean

Pacific Ocean

Africa

South America

Range

Indian Ocean

N
W ⬌ E
S

Australia

Southern Ocean

They can live in different **habitats**. Some live in woodlands and forests. Others live in swamps. They all find homes near water.

Quokkas rest all day. It can get very hot. They tunnel through brush and thick grass. It gives them shade from the sun. It's a good place to hide from **predators** too.

Quokkas are most active at night. It's cooler then. They come out of hiding to eat. They spend most of their time on the ground. But they can climb trees to reach food. They may also climb to escape danger.

Happy Hoppers

People once thought quokkas were giant rats. Four hundred years ago, a Dutch explorer landed on Rottnest Island. He saw the animals and their long tails. He named the island after them. In Dutch it means "rat's nest."

But these cute animals are more like kangaroos than rats. Their front legs are very short. They use their front paws to pick up food. Their back legs are long and strong. They use them for hopping. That is how they move around.

Quokkas have thick, brownish gray fur. It blends in with the grass. The fur covers almost everything but their tails. Their ears are short and round. They have black noses.

These animals are about the same size as cats. They grow up to 21 inches (53 centimeters) long. They weigh up to 9 pounds (4.1 kilograms). Males are usually bigger than females.

Females have pouches. They are used to carry around their young.

Quokkas have sharp claws on their feet. They help them to climb trees. They use them to fight off attacks too.

And don't forget about those sweet smiles! They always look like they are smiling. But they are actually **panting**. This fast breathing helps to keep them cool on hot days.

On the Menu

Quokkas eat leaves and grass. They eat bark and stems too. They don't chew their food right away. They swallow it whole. Later, they bring it back up. They chew it and swallow it again.

At night, they gather in big groups around water holes. But they only drink if they are very thirsty. They get most of their water from the plants they eat.

Quokkas live where it gets very hot. These places go through dry seasons. There is very little rain. Water may dry up.

Sometimes food is hard to find too. But quokkas can go months without food and water. They store fat in their tails. When they can't eat they live off the fat.

Life of a Quokka

Quokkas live in family groups. There can be between 20 and 150 in a group.

On the mainland, these animals **mate** during summer. Sometimes females have two babies during a year. On Rottnest Island they only mate between January and March.

About one month after mating, a female gives birth to one baby. A baby is called a joey. It is pink and hairless when its born. It is blind too.

The baby crawls into its mother's pouch. It drinks milk from its mother. She keeps the baby warm and safe. It stays in the pouch for about six months.

After coming out of the pouch, young quokkas stay close to their mothers. They learn how to find food. But if they are scared, they jump back in the pouch.

After around a year, quokkas can live on their own. Some stay in the group with their mothers. Others will leave to join another group. They can have babies of their own at 18 months old. They can live up to 10 years.

Dangers to Quokkas

The quokkas that live on the mainland of Australia have a few predators. Foxes, dogs, and cats attack them. These animals don't live on the islands. Quokkas are safer there. But they face other dangers. Wildfires can happen during the dry season.

Humans are also a threat. Forests are being cut down. The quokkas are losing their homes. People visiting the island feed them. It can make them sick.

The number of quokkas is going down. But people are working to help them. Groups are trying to control wild animals that attack them. Laws have also been put in place. They protect the land they live on. People want to make sure these happy animals are around for many years to come.

Fast Facts

Name: quokka

Habitat: woodlands, forests, swamps

Where in the World: western Australia, Rottnest Island, Bald Island

Food: leaves, grass, stems, bark

Predators: dogs, cats, foxes

Life span: up to 10 years

Glossary

habitat (HAB-uh-tat)—the natural place and conditions in which a plant or animal lives

mammal (MAM-uhl)—a warm–blooded animal that breathes air; mammals have hair or fur; female mammals feed milk to their young

marsupial (mar-SOO-pee-uhl)—an animal that carries its young in a pouch

mate (MATE)—to join with another to produce young

pant (PANT)—to breathe quickly with an open mouth; some animals pant to cool off

predator (PRED-uh-tur)—an animal that hunts other animals for food

Read More

Hansen, Grace. *Quokka*. Minneapolis: Abdo Kids, 2020.

Jenner, Caryn. *Meet the Quokkas!* New York: DK Publishing, 2020.

Rustad, Martha, E. H. *Baby Animals in Pouches*. North Mankato, MN: Capstone Press, 2017.

Internet Sites

CBC Kids–Fun Facts About Cute Animals
cbc.ca/kidscbc2/the-feed/fun-facts-about-cute-animals-quokka-edition

Kiddle–Quokka Facts for Kids
kids.kiddle.co/Quokka

Rottnest Is Wildlife–Quokka
wildlife.rottnestisland.com/land/fauna/quokka

Index